How to Be a BiBLe

Beauty

How to Be a

Bible Beauty

Catherine Mackenzie

CF4•K

Dedication:
For all my nieces and my nearly nieces :-)

10 9 8 7 6 5 4 3 2 1

© Copyright 2015 Catherine Mackenzie
ISBN: 978-1-78191-578-3

Published by
Christian Focus Publications,
Geanies House, Fearn, Tain, Ross-shire, IV20 1TW, U.K.

Cover design by Daniel van Straaten
Illustrations by Jeff Anderson
Printed and bound by Nørhaven, Denmark

CONTENTS

What is Beauty?.. 7

Rebekah's Beauty..................................... 17

Rebekah's Rebellion.............................. 33

Leah's Love... 45

Ruth's Redemption 59

Martha and Mary..................................... 75

Perfume and Tears.................................. 89

Darling Dorcas... 99

Ruby and You... 109

What is a Princess?................................ 119

Who is Catherine Mackenzie?............. 124

What is Beauty?

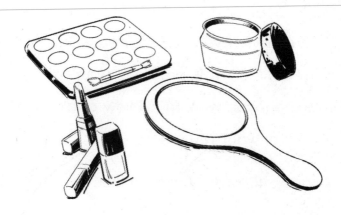

Have you ever sat down at your dressing table and said the following words: 'Mirror, mirror on the wall, who's the fairest of them all?'

And has your mirror ever answered you back?

(Of course not!) What would you do if it did?

A. Scream in fright?

B. Throw it out the window?

C. Start an argument with it – 'Hey you mirror! You've got a cheek. You're not so hot looking yourself with that 1980s framing! You're so last century!'?

If you have ever had a conversation with your mirror then you probably won't admit to it. Imagine if you were in full flow and someone walked in on you! You'd never live it down.

Anyway, the line 'Mirror, mirror, on the wall' is from the fairy story *Snow White* where an enchanted mirror can tell you if you are the fairest in all the land.

Now, I don't believe in talking mirrors or flying fairies! Neither should you. But let's have a bit of fun and imagine that a ridiculous looking woman, with purple wings on her back, comes to visit for afternoon tea. Along with a packet of biscuits, she brings you a parcel in shiny paper, with a label on the side. On the label are the words, 'Whatever is inside this parcel will make you beautiful.' What would you hope to get?

A. Bouncy blonde curls?

B. Straight black locks?

C. Tiny feet?

D. A long neck?

E. A little nose?

F. A tan?

That's quite a list isn't it? But this list could go on and on as every country and each century has its own idea about what is 'stunning' or 'gorgeous'.

Ladies in Victorian times never went outside without a hat. If their skin went brown in the sun it was considered unattractive. This was because a tanned skin said certain things about the way you lived. It meant that you spent a lot of time outdoors – and probably had to work for your living. A pale complexion meant you were 'well off' and from a 'better class of people'.

After some time had passed people changed their opinion: they wanted to look tanned instead of pale. It was considered 'attractive' – because it meant you were one of those rich people who could afford to travel and go to sunny climates to laze about on the beach all day.

And then there's the Bible – beauty is described in different ways there too. The Song of Solomon describes a young woman by saying, 'Behold you are fair, my love! Behold you are fair! You have dove's eyes behind your veil. Your hair is like a flock of goats going down from Mount Gilead. Your teeth are like a flock of shorn sheep.'

Different times and different cultures saw different things as being beautiful.

But the beauty that the Bible is really telling us about is a lot more than our skin and bones or even our hair and teeth. Physical beauty is temporary at its best. The Bible wants us to be spiritually beautiful, because that beauty reflects God's beauty and it is eternal.

The Bible tells us in Proverbs 31:30 that beauty is 'passing'. That means it is here one day and gone the next. The physical beauty you have as a young woman disappears as you get older. This sort of beauty is just skin deep as they say – it only lasts a short time. It's not going to give you long term happiness. And even if you did look physically 'goooorrrrgeous' all of your life – it wouldn't give you true joy. Some people think it would – but they'd be wrong. Some people worry about looking 'just right' – but this sort of worrying is such a waste of time.

Don't get me wrong. It's good to brush your hair, wash your face and wear smart clothes – it's just not the be-all-and-end-all. It's certainly not something to worry about because the Bible says that we're not to worry about these things!

Read more: Matthew 6:25-34

Do you spend a lot of time and thought on making yourself physically beautiful? Is it important that you always have the most up to date fashions? If you could, would you change your nose, your height, your eye colour, your shape?

Here's an interesting Bible fact: None of us, by being anxious, can even add an hour to our lives or even a few inches to our height! The Bible also tells us not to worry about what we are going to wear!

This summer I went for a walk in the country and saw the most gorgeous array of lilies floating in a lake. They were stunning. Pale petals, as pale as any Victorian lady could have wished for. A light pink blush was in the centre of each of them – as subtle and breathtaking as any make-up artist could ever achieve. And here's the thing –

God did that! The Bible tells us in Matthew 6 that the lilies don't work but not even the greatest king in the world was ever dressed as beautifully as them. So if God takes care of lilies like this – he's going to take care of you! Don't spend time stressing about the way you look. Trust in God. He provides.

Think instead about a different kind of beauty … it's a biblical beauty. It lasts for ever. It gives you real happiness because this beauty is Jesus Christ himself! Breathtaking! He is the most beautiful Person in the Bible, in the world, in all of creation – Jesus Christ, the Son of God and the Son of Man, the Saviour, the Prince of Peace, the King of kings and Lord of lords.

Jesus did not have what we would call 'film-star' looks. We are told in Isaiah 53:2 that Jesus wasn't really anything special to look at. He had a body like anyone else, he grew up physically like anyone else, but he 'had no form or majesty that we should look at him or beauty that we should desire him.' (ESV)

So how is it that Jesus is the most beautiful? Well, it's simply that the beauty of Christ is something far greater and far more lovely than anything you will ever see on a magazine. His beauty is holy. It's perfect. Think about these words: Love, joy, peace, kindness, goodness, gentleness, faithfulness, self Control.

You don't see these words in a mirror. But, you see them in every single way in Jesus Christ. Each of these words is Jesus. Jesus is each of these words. In absolutely every way.

And these are words that God gives his people. Those who trust in the Lord receive so many good gifts from God their Father. Along with salvation, forgiveness of sin and eternal life, God gives his children true eternal beauty. This is the beauty that we're going to find out about. So stop chatting to that mirror of yours and start reading ....

ReBeKah's BeauTy

Do you like romance? Do you like it when the guy gets the girl in the movie? When he 'pops the question' to his leading lady – what kind of proposal scene would you give top marks to?

A. He sends the girl a letter, drenched in perfume, with a silk ribbon attached (Jane Austen style).

B. He gets down on bended knee in a restaurant with a ring (Probably the way most guys do it).

C. A servant is sent to get a young man a wife from a far away village. He arrives with a pile of camels and the girl is expected to give them as much water as they can drink. ... Uh-huh! You read that right.

Letter C is a genuine real life biblical proposal, and it happened to a girl called Rebekah.

Camels, water and a well? What do they teach us about beauty? Well, this story tells us that a woman's beauty should be more than decorative. A woman can also have muscle and common sense! But more importantly this story also tells us that real beauty is about God's plans and how they are the best plans!

So let's meet Rebekah ... She lived during a time, after the flood, when humanity had started to speak many different languages. The people of the world had become so self-important that God had to put them in their place. He deliberately confused them by giving them different languages. It was also part of God's plan to choose one of these people groups to be given the truth of God's Word. God chose a man called Abram who would be the first of God's chosen people, the Hebrews. After a very long wait, Abram and his wife Sarai finally had a son called Isaac. Rebekah would eventually become Isaac's wife and this is where our story begins ...

Isaac's mother had just died and he was naturally very sad about this. Abram, who was now called Abraham, realised that it was time for his son to get married so he decided to do something about it. After he had buried his wife, he took his chief servant aside and asked him to promise him something. The servant was to return to Abraham's homeland to get Isaac a wife.

19

Abraham was very concerned that the right sort of girl was chosen. But he couldn't go off and do this sort of thing himself, as he was now very old. He simply had to entrust this task to someone else. Who better than his most trusted servant?

The servant, however, was concerned about how he was actually going to achieve this. He must have known a bit about women because he said to Abraham, 'Perhaps she will not be willing to follow me? I might have to take your son with me.'

The servant obviously thought that most girls would want to at least see their potential husband first before marrying him.

However, Abraham was having none of that! 'Do not take my son back there!' he exclaimed.

Though Abraham wanted his son to marry a girl from his homeland, he did not want Isaac, his one and only son, to return to that place.

Abraham tried to comfort his servant by saying, 'The Lord God of heaven will send his angel before you and you shall take a wife for my son from there.'

That was that! So the servant made his promise to Abraham and with ten of his master's camels, he set off on his journey to the land of Mesopotamia to the city of Nahor.

When he arrived he wasn't really sure about what to do. He was in the right area, but how was he to meet the right girl? God gave him an idea. It was time for the women to come out from their homes to the well to get water. So once he had got his camels to kneel down nearby, he prayed to God, 'O Lord God of my master, Abraham, please give me success this day and show kindness to my master Abraham. Behold, here I stand by this well of water and the daughters of the city are coming out to draw water.

'Now, may it be that the young woman to whom I say, "Please set down your pitcher that I may drink," and she says, "Drink and I will also give your camels a drink" – let her be the one you have appointed for your servant Isaac. And by this I will know that you have shown kindness to my master.'

Just before he had finished speaking, a young woman appeared. She had in her arms a water jar and she was also beautiful to look at.

The servant came up to this girl and said, 'Please let me drink a little water from your pitcher.'

I wonder what he thought when she replied, 'Drink, my Lord, and I will draw water for your camels also, until they have finished drinking.'

The servant must have been
1. Astonished
2. Excited
3. Thankful

He was probably all three!

The servant watched as she made many journeys back and fore to the well to fill up the water trough for the ten camels. Now a camel can drink twenty-five gallons of water in ten minutes. So Rebekah had a lot of work to do, especially if the camels were really thirsty and hadn't had a drink in a while. This would have been a physically demanding job for Rebekah. But she did it! Every single one of the camels drank its fill. The servant came up to young Rebekah and gave her a golden nose ring and two bracelets and said, 'Whose daughter are you? Tell me, please, is there room for me to stay in your father's house?'

'I am the daughter of Bethuel, Milcah's son whom she bore to Nahor. You can stay with us. We have more than enough room.'

The servant was so overwhelmed by what the young woman had just said, he immediately bowed down and worshipped God. He realised that God had guided him right to the house of Abraham's own relatives. Rebekah ran back to her home to tell her family all that had happened.

Rebekah's brother Laban came out to see what she was talking about. As soon as he met the servant, he ushered him inside the house and made sure that his camels were well looked after too.

Food was set before the servant, but before he ate, he insisted on telling the family about the reason for his journey.

'I will not eat until I have told you about my errand. I am Abraham's servant. The Lord has blessed my master greatly. Sarah, my master's wife, bore a son to my master when she was old and to him he has given all that he has. Now my master made me swear saying, "You shall not take a wife for my son from the Canaanites in whose land I dwell, but you shall go to my father's house and to my family and take a wife for my son." And I said to my master, "Perhaps the woman will not follow me." But Abraham said to me, "The Lord before whom I walk will send his angel with you and prosper your way and you shall take a wife for my son from my father's house."

'And this day I came to the well and said to the Lord, "Let it be that the young woman to whom I say, 'Please set down your pitcher that I may drink', and she says, 'Drink and I will also give your camels a drink' let her be the one you have appointed for your servant Isaac."

'But before I had finished speaking in my heart there was Rebekah coming out with her water pitcher on her shoulder. When I asked her for a drink, she made haste and set down her pitcher and said, "Drink and I will give your camels a drink also."

'So I drank and she gave the camels a drink too. I asked her whose daughter she was and she said, "The daughter of Bethuel, Nahor's son, whom Milcah bore to him."'

The servant then asked Rebekah's family to give their daughter to Isaac to be his wife.

Rebekah's father and brother gave their permission. The following day they asked Rebekah personally what she wanted to do.

'Will you go with this man?' they asked.

Rebekah replied, 'I will go.'

So Rebekah then made the journey to a land that she had never seen and to Isaac, a man that she had never met.

As Isaac was out walking and thinking in the field one evening, he saw in the distance some camels coming towards him. He began to walk towards them.

Rebekah also saw Isaac in the distance and asked the servant who he was. When she heard that he was the man she was to marry, she covered her face with a veil and Isaac brought her into the tent that had once been his mother's.

She was now his wife and he loved her.

Rebekah's love story is an amazing one. She was God's chosen woman for Isaac, but the real beauty of this love story is the fact that God is at the centre of it, directing the servant and directing Rebekah in everything.

Read More: Genesis 24

The Lord God is amazing. He is omnipotent – all powerful, omniscient – all knowing. He is sovereign and in control of everything. He is in control even when we go against him. Going against God is something that Rebekah did later in her life.

Beauty Tips

If you want to have real beauty, you need to be beautiful in God's way. That means to be beautiful in your spirit – or inside. To have godly beauty means that you follow God's law, love him and trust him – giving him the highest importance in your life. However, every human being is a sinner. They are in rebellion against God. If human beings were left to their own devices they would always chose to hurt others and put themselves first. The Bible tells us that 'All have sinned' and that we all 'fall short' of God's perfect, beautiful, standard.

Think about Jesus

So is there any hope? Our sin separates us from God and keeps us out of heaven. That's what we deserve. But God in his beautiful, perfect, merciful love planned a rescue from the very beginning. Jesus Christ, God's Son, was sent to this world as a human being to live the perfect life that no other human being could live. He willingly went to the cross and died. When he was on the cross he took the punishment for sin. When we trust in Jesus Christ to cleanse us from sin and trust in God to forgive us, God takes Jesus Christ's beautiful righteousness and puts it on us. On the cross, God took our ugly sin and put it on Christ. Christ's beauty is given to sinners. What an exchange!

Read More: Romans 3:23, Luke 23.

GODLY BEAUTY

One thing have I asked of the LORD, that will I seek after: that I may dwell in the house of the LORD all the days of my life, to gaze upon the beauty of the LORD and to inquire in his temple. Psalm 27:4 (ESV)

How is God beautiful? Forget those magazines and their mediocre descriptions of beauty. God's beauty stops you in your tracks and makes you gasp. It gives you a pure, eternal, heart-thumping joy! When we see snow-capped mountains,

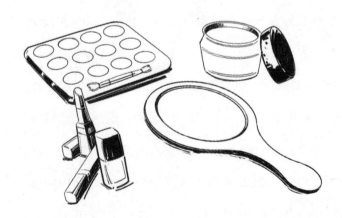

intricate flowers, a charging horse, a cell under a microscope, a star through a telescope – these are amazing, beautiful even. They are, however, a pale reflection of the beauty of their Creator who, with the power of his word, brought everything in this world into being. So look back at Psalm 27:4. The one who wrote this Psalm longs to spend time with the Lord. He wants to find out more about him. One way for us to do this is by going to church – but it must be a church where God's Word is preached, where the people read God's Word and believe it and obey it. Are you part of God's church or are you just someone who goes because you're told to? Is church something you do at Christmas and Easter and the occasional wedding? If that's all God means to you then you don't really appreciate his beauty. You're not gazing on the beauty of the Lord; you're just taking an occasional peek, if that. Those who love the beauty of God, long to hear the Word preached. When you love God's beauty, you will be thrilled when you read the Bible and see Jesus in every page.

ReBekah's ReBellioN

an you expect good results if you don't follow the instructions? For example;

1. You're going to bake a cake. But instead of following the recipe, you decide to miss out a few ingredients. 'I don't have any sugar, or eggs either. But that won't matter much.'

2. You decide to mend a car engine. 'I've never done it before and I can't be bothered reading that manual, but how hard can it be?'

3. You meet a Martian and decide it would be a good idea to teach him how to knit. You don't know how to knit and you don't speak Martian either. 'I don't need to learn his language! If I speak loud enough in a foreign accent, he is bound to understand. Even if he is an alien.'

All three of these scenarios are recipes for disaster! It's never going to work.

Rebekah and her husband Isaac should have listened to God's instructions and trusted him too. But they didn't! Family Feud Alert!!!

Rebekah and her husband Isaac found out that they were going to have twins. Rebekah was concerned because the two children seemed to be struggling and fighting with each other inside her womb. She took her concerns to the Lord God who told her, 'Two nations are in your womb, two peoples shall be separated from your body; One people shall be stronger than the other and the older shall serve the younger.'

This was an important message. It was unusual for an older child to be less important than the younger. But, somehow, this message got ignored, and as a result there was great trouble in the family.

Rebekah gave birth to two very different boys. Esau, the oldest, was red and hairy and grew up to be an outdoors type of guy. Jacob, was smooth-skinned and grew up to be a quiet man preferring to remain at home.

Sadly, both Isaac and Rebekah made the mistake of loving one son more than the other. Isaac loved Esau best and Rebekah loved Jacob.

When Isaac grew old and his eyesight had grown dim he decided that he wanted to give a special blessing to his oldest son. He called Esau to him and said, 'I don't know when I am going to die, so please take your weapons and hunt some game for me. Then make my favourite stew and I will bless you before I die.'

Rebekah overheard this and when Esau had left, she immediately went to speak with Jacob.

'Your father has instructed Esau, your brother, to hunt some game and then cook him a savoury stew before he gives him a blessing. Listen to me

then and do what you are told. Go to the flock and bring me two of the best young goats and I will make a stew for your father, just the way he likes it. Then you will take it to your father and he will bless you before he dies.'

This is where the love story of Rebekah and Isaac starts to look ugly, rather than beautiful.

Isaac chose to ignore the word that God had given his wife during her pregnancy. He chose to bless Esau when God had clearly said that the oldest son was to serve the youngest.

Rebekah chose not to trust the Lord with Jacob's future. Instead she chose to disobey God and deceive her husband by tricking him into blessing Jacob rather than Esau.

What a mess! But how did Rebekah plan for this trick to work? Jacob pointed out that even though his father was blind, he'd be able to tell that it was Jacob and not Esau. 'My brother is a

37

hairy man,' Jacob explained 'and I am smooth-skinned. Perhaps my father will feel me and he will realise that I am a liar. He will curse me rather than bless me.'

Rebekah, however, had it all worked out. She told Jacob to get the meat and leave the rest up to her. Jacob did so. Rebekah cooked the stew and then she took Esau's clothes and put them on Jacob. She took the skins of the goats she had just butchered and put these on the hands and neck of Jacob. Jacob then took the stew to his father and said, 'I am Esau your firstborn. I have done just as you told me. Please eat the meat that I have prepared for you so that you may bless me.'

Lie Number One! The deception was in full swing.

But Isaac was puzzled. It hadn't been that long since Esau had left. 'How did you find the game so quickly my son?' he asked.

Jacob replied, 'God brought it to me.'

Lie Number Two! The deception was at a whole new level! Jacob had even used God's name.

However, Isaac was still a bit suspicious. He reached out to touch his son's arm – it felt hairy. 'The voice is Jacob's,' he muttered. 'But the hands are the hands of Esau.'

'Are you really my son Esau?' Isaac asked.

Jacob lied once again, 'I am.'

Lie Number Three! So Isaac ate the stew and drank and then he blessed his youngest son.

'May God give you the dew of heaven and of the fatness of the earth, and plenty of grain and wine. Let peoples serve you, and nations bow down to you. Be master over your brethren and let your mother's sons bow down to you. Cursed be everyone who curses you, and blessed be those who bless you!'

Later, when Esau returned and he and Isaac discovered the deception, Esau was livid! He begged his father to bless him too, but the only blessing that Isaac could give his oldest son was hardly anything in comparison to what he had already given Jacob.

Esau vowed to kill his brother and when Rebekah heard of his plans, she warned Jacob and urged him to go to stay with her brother Laban until Esau's anger had calmed down.

So because Isaac and Rebekah had not followed God's Word, had not trusted in him and instead had gone their own way – their family was divided. Favouritism and deception had infected their family. But be careful! It is easy to judge them when we shouldn't. After all, would you and I have behaved differently in the same situation? Remember, Rebekah and Isaac were sinners - and so are we. Obedience and trust in God are beautiful. Disobedience, deception and sin are ugly. God's plan to have the older son serve the younger still came to pass. He is always in control of everything.

GODLY BEAUTY

But I have trusted in your steadfast love; my heart shall rejoice in your salvation. Psalm 13:5 (ESV)

Love is beautiful. It is a shame that the story of Rebekah and Isaac doesn't have more love in it than it does. The love that Rebekah showed Jacob and the love that Isaac showed Esau wasn't really love – it was favouritism. It was choosing one son above the other and that's not real love. There's a word for that kind of favouritism. It's called partiality. And the Bible has quite a bit to say about that. Look up the following Bible verses:

Read More: James 2:1&9; Romans 2:11

So what does the Bible say about love? The Bible has loads to say about love. It tells us that God is love three times in the book of 1 John.

Read More: 1 John 4:7, 8 & 16

In the book of Psalms God's love is often described as steadfast. That's a word that means you can trust God's love. He doesn't profess to love you one moment and then forget you the next.

Beauty Tips

The Bible tells us that we're to love others as much as we love ourselves and we are even to love our enemies. But we're to love God most of all.

Read More: Matthew 12:33; Luke 6:32

The love that we are to show is like the love that God has shown to us. While we were still sinners and his enemies, Christ died for us.

Read More: Romans 5:8

So to be truly beautiful we have to be a reflection of God's eternal beauty. We are to show the love of God by loving him first and loving others – even those who hate us.

Think about Jesus

What love Jesus showed to sinners when he died in their place on the cross! The Bible tells us that there is no greater love than the love someone shows when they give their life for their friends. Jesus gave up his life for his enemies! Because that is what sinners are; they are the enemies of God. It is only the power of God that can transform an enemy of God into a friend. The Bible says in John 3:16 that 'God so loved the world that he gave his one and only son so that whoever believes in him should not perish but have eternal life.' What love! There is no greater friend than that!

Read More: 1 John 4:19

Leah's Love

n the movies, especially romances, there is always a hero and a heroine ... and the two get together usually because of something remarkable that takes place. In a typical movie romance the hero or heroine may do something brave, spectacular or just simply breathtaking.

What kind of incredible feat would your movie hero have to do to get his gal?

1. Rescue a helpless kitten from a burning multistorey building, while writing his speech for receiving his Nobel Peace Prize.

2. Knock out a giant gorilla while composing a love sonnet and strumming a guitar.

3. Push away a big heavy stone so the heroine can water her sheep – sobbing his heart out while he does it.

Uh-huh! You've guessed it. Number three isn't in the movies – it's in the Bible! This is the way that Jacob first met the girl of his dreams.

So how does Jacob end up falling in love? When we read about him last he was running away from a very hairy and angry big brother! Well, on Rebekah's advice, Jacob fled to his relatives to escape Esau's wrath. Rebekah had suggested that her brother, Laban, would be a good person to help Jacob out at least until Esau's anger had cooled down a bit.

So Jacob ran for his life! When he got near to Laban's land, he came across a well and some shepherds. The custom was that the well was not opened until all the local flocks had arrived. It was only at that point that one of the shepherds would move the stone. Jacob asked about his uncle Laban and just then he was pointed towards a young woman and a flock of sheep making their way towards them. 'That's Laban's daughter Rachel.' Jacob tried to persuade the shepherds to let Rachel water her flocks there and then, but they wouldn't. So Jacob went and rolled away the stone and watered Rachel's sheep for her. Jacob was pretty emotional. He was, after all, far away from his homeland and it must have been something special to actually meet a member of his family.

As soon as Rachel realised that Jacob was Rebekah's son, she ran to fetch her father. And this is how the romance began. Rachel was beautiful in form and appearance. Jacob was smitten! Rachel did have an older sister, named Leah, but Leah was not as physically attractive as her younger sister. Jacob firmly set his heart on Rachel and agreed to work for Laban for seven years, if Rachel would be given to him as his wife at the end of that time. Laban agreed and Jacob was delighted and the seven years felt like only a few days because Jacob was so in love.

But the next bit of the story was not what Jacob would have expected! Remember how he had been part of a shameful deception. He had gone along with his mother's plot to trick Jacob's elderly blind father ... a dreadful lie. Well, now Jacob was going to be on the receiving end of just this same sort of treatment. He was going to get a taste of his own medicine!

Seven years had passed and Jacob reminded Laban of his promise to let Rachel become his wife. The wedding day was set. It was the custom in those days for the bride to wear a veil. Jacob would not have been able to see his bride's face during the wedding ceremony. It wasn't a big deal, every bride wore a veil on her wedding day. Jacob would have thought nothing of it!

However, the bride was not what she appeared to be – in fact she was someone completely different. On the wedding day Laban took his oldest daughter, Leah, and gave her to Jacob instead of Rachel. The veil was a cunning disguise! It was only on the morning after the wedding that Jacob realised that he had been tricked into marrying a woman he didn't love.

'What have you done to me?' he yelled at Laban. 'Why have you lied to me?'

Laban's excuse was, 'In our country we never let the younger daughter marry first. Stay with Leah for the wedding week and then you can marry Rachel too ... as long as you work for me for another seven years.'

The whole situation was a mess. That is what sin and lies and disobedience to God do to our lives, our families and our world. God's plan and purpose for the world was clearly shown in the Garden of Eden – one man and one woman. That is what marriage is supposed to be. God created Adam and then he created Eve to be his wife. But sin came into the world and marriage was one of the good plans of God that got spoiled by humanity's sin. Right up to the present day couples separate, divorce, and cheat on each other by loving other men's wives and other women's husbands.

Jacob was no different. He loved Rachel. He paid no regard to the law of God. He wanted Rachel for himself so he would have her no matter what. Jacob was already married to Leah, but he went ahead and married Rachel too. It was wrong of Laban to deceive Jacob, but it was wrong of Jacob to have two wives at the same time. So much heartache, division and jealousy came into Jacob's family because of his actions.

You see, Jacob loved Rachel and didn't love Leah. Jealousy sprang up between the women. Because God saw that Leah was unloved he gave her children. When Rachel eventually had two sons, Jacob again showed favouritism to them over Leah's children. The jealousy increased because of the sin that was in the hearts of the whole family. But even though Leah was jealous of her sister and continued to sin throughout her life, she learned about true beauty and love. She learned that these came from God.

Initially, every time that Leah gave birth, she longed for Jacob to love her in the way he loved Rachel.

'God has seen my sadness. Surely my husband will love me now.'

'Now at last my husband will become attached to me. I have given him three sons.'

Then something beautiful happened. When she gave birth to her fourth son, Leah's attitude changed. 'This time I will praise the Lord!' she exclaimed as she held her new born baby, Judah, in her arms.

She must have longed for the love of her husband, but Leah was brought to realise that the love of God was more loving and more beautiful than any love from any man.

Jacob's family was definitely mixed up. Sin had spoiled so much. But even with all that, God still used this family for his great plan. Leah's son, Judah, is in the family tree of Jesus Christ, the Son of God. You can read Jesus' family tree in the first chapter of Matthew. Leah wasn't the most beautiful, her husband didn't love her, sin in her life and the lives of others in her family caused great pain, but she was chosen by God to give birth to a son who would be an ancestor of Christ, the Saviour of sinners.

And then Rachel's life was used by God too. Though she died giving birth to her second son, Benjamin, Rachel's first born son, Joseph, was used by God to save their whole family, and many other families too. But that's another story for another time. You can read it for yourself in Genesis 37–50.

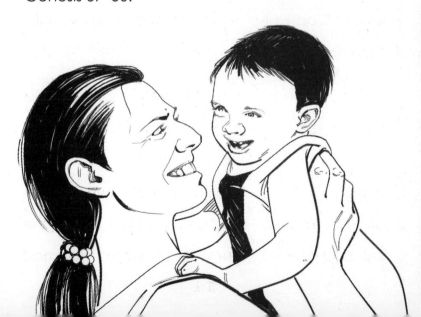

Beauty Tips

Here are two Bible beauty words: Joy and Peace. There doesn't seem to be much of either in the family life of Jacob. But Leah eventually shows real joy and praises God for his love and his kindness. The main purpose of our lives is to glorify God and enjoy him. It is not to be physically beautiful. The apostle Paul said to Timothy in his letter 'while bodily training is of some value, godliness is of value in every way, as it holds promise for the present life and also for the life to come' 1 Timothy 4:8.

Love, joy and peace are what real beauty is. When we are joyful, we are more than just happy. Joy is a deep, eternal gladness in our heart that God gives us even when things don't go our way. Joy is a gladness that we have because of what God has done for us in sending his Son to this world to save sinners.

Read More: Psalm 16:11; Psalm 21:6; Romans 15:13; James 1:2; Psalm 34:14; Matthew 5:9; Romans 5:1; Romans 12:18; Ephesians 2:14.

GoDLY BeaUtY

Do not let your adorning be external—the braiding of hair and the putting on of gold jewellery, or the clothing you wear—but let your adorning be the hidden person of the heart with the imperishable beauty of a gentle and quiet spirit, which in God's sight is very precious.
1 Peter 3:3-4 (ESV)

This is very good advice about godly beauty. Peter was writing to the church and in these verses he speaks directly to the women of the church.

So when you sit at your mirror in the morning, devote some time to God while you get yourself ready. It's far more important. Because the things of God are eternal and last forever and the things of this world are only temporary and pass away.

Are you a follower of Jesus Christ? Well then, when people meet you they should be amazed at how loving and joyful and peaceful you are. If you love Jesus, your life should show others the love, joy and peace of God. Your life should not be about you or how beautiful you look – it should be about God and how lovely he is!

Think about Jesus

If anyone deserved to wear expensive clothes – it was Jesus. If anyone deserved riches – it was Jesus. If anyone deserved to be exalted as the most important person ever – it was Jesus. He is the Son of God after all. Yes, he is the King of kings and Lord of lords, the Prince of Peace but he is different to the rulers and authorities we see in this world. He is also the 'Suffering servant'. He shows us through his life and death that the Kingdom of Heaven is different to the Kingdom of this world. Sinful people want to lord it over others. Jesus, the only one who deserves to be exalted actually humbled himself. He gave himself to others. He healed the sick. He showed love to the down-trodden and despised. He even did tasks that others considered beneath them. And then he humbled himself by submitting to a disgraceful death on a cross – all to save sinners from the punishment of guilt and sin.

Read More: Matthew 20: 24-26; Philippians 2:8

Ruth's Redemption

Traditionally men are the ones who ask women to marry them. But this isn't always the case. The story we are going to read about now has quite a different sort of proposal in it – so be warned! God planned that this time a woman would be the one popping the question. In fact, there were two women involved in this marriage proposal ... but more about that later. Let's start off with a question for you - If you wanted to propose to the man of your dreams how would you go about it?

1. Go down on bended knee in a restaurant (The way most guys do it).

2. Bake him a great big cake and then shout, 'Marry me' really loudly. Be careful though, he might choke in shock and swallow the engagement ring you hid in the second slice.

3. Make sure that he gets really cold feet and can't go to sleep!

Well – again – number three is a strange one! But truth is stranger than fiction they say! And one girl in the Bible does actually propose marriage in this rather peculiar way. This girl's name was Ruth.

She is the heroine of our story, but as is the case in all Bible stories, this story isn't really about Ruth – this story is about God. Yes, we have a romance here, a love story, but it's God's love story; the love story between God and his people.

In the days before the land of Israel had a king of its own, there was a famine. It was serious and so bad that it forced a family to leave their home in Bethlehem to flee to the land of Moab, where there was food. Elimelech and his wife Naomi took their two sons, Mahlon and Kilion, away from their homeland. It was a big decision, but in time the family settled in this foreign land and the two boys even married local women, one called Ruth and the other Orpah. However, tragedy struck. First, Elimelech died and then his two sons. Naomi and her two daughters-in-law were left without any male protection. During those times women were vulnerable on their own. It was hard, if not impossible, for them to make a living without having a husband or son to look after them. When Naomi heard that the famine in the land of Israel had ended, she decided to return home.

Ruth and Orpah wanted to come with her. But Naomi felt that it wasn't fair to ask these two young women to leave their homeland. She tried to persuade them to stay behind with their own people, to find new husbands and settle down.

Both Ruth and Orpah wept aloud at the thought of leaving Naomi. But Naomi insisted 'Go home my daughters. I am not going to have any more sons who could become your husbands! I am too old for another husband myself and even if I was young enough and gave birth to sons, would you wait until they grew up?'

At this Orpah said goodbye, but Ruth clung to Naomi. Naomi urged Ruth to follow Orpah, but Ruth replied, 'Don't urge me to leave you or to turn back from you. Where you go, I will go and where you stay, I will stay. Your people will be my people and your God my God. Where you die, I will die and there I will be buried. May the Lord deal with me, be it ever so severely if anything but death separates you and me.'

Ruth loved the one true God and had placed her trust in him. With Ruth's heart set on the Lord there was nothing that Naomi could say to separate them. So, together, Ruth and Naomi left Moab and returned to the land of Israel, back to the people of God. And it was just in time for the harvest.

This was good timing for the two women. During harvest-time it was the custom to allow people who were in poverty to gather up the left-over grain in the fields. This was called gleaning. Sometimes seeds and stalks of grain would be left behind as the harvest was gathered in. The very poorest people were allowed into the field to gather what they could. From these meagre gatherings they would try and keep hunger at bay.

Ruth soon realised that this was going to be the only way to stop Naomi and herself from starving. And, as it turned out, Ruth ended up working in a field belonging to a man called Boaz, a relative of Naomi's dead husband, Elimelech.

When Boaz arrived in the field and saw Ruth hard at work, he asked one of his men, 'Whose young woman is that?'

His foreman replied, 'She is the girl from Moab who came back with Naomi. She asked permission to gather grain and has been working steadily from morning.'

When Boaz realised who she was, he approached her. 'Daughter, listen to me. Stay in my fields with my servant girls. I've told my men not to bother you. Don't go anywhere else and whenever you are thirsty, drink from the water jugs my men have filled. '

Ruth was overwhelmed at his generosity and

kindness. 'Why have I found such favour in your eyes? I'm only a foreigner.'

Boaz replied, 'I know what you have done for your mother-in-law, Naomi, since her husband died. May the Lord repay you for what you have done. May you be richly rewarded by the Lord, the God of Israel, under whose wings you have come to take refuge.'

For the rest of the day Boaz looked out for Ruth. At meal-time he made sure she had plenty to eat. He gave special instructions to his men to make sure they let her gather grain anywhere in the field. They were even told to pull out stalks from the harvest sheaves and leave them for Ruth to pick up. At the end of the day Ruth's pile of grain was quite substantial.

Naomi was overjoyed when Ruth came home with such a big pile of grain. 'Where did you glean today?' she asked.

Ruth replied, 'The name of the man I worked with today is Boaz.'

'The Lord bless him!' Naomi cried out. 'This man is a close relative. He is a Kinsmen Redeemer. It will be good for you to work there,' Naomi said.

So Ruth did exactly that. She worked in Boaz's fields until the barley and wheat harvests were finished.

But why was Naomi so pleased Ruth was working in Boaz's fields? And what exactly was a kinsman-redeemer?

We all know that Naomi was poor, but she did own land. It was just that her husband had taken the family away from their land when the famine had hit. Their fields had not yielded any crops. Nothing had grown there in the time that they had been away. Land needs people to plant and harvest and look after the soil and crops. Naomi had returned to fields that had not been planted, that could not be harvested and that she, as an elderly woman, could not look after. The land, however, still belonged to her husband and would have belonged to her sons if they had lived. There was one way and one way only that she could get money for the land and still keep the land in the family. Close male relatives could buy the land from her and if the male relative was single, he was also obliged to marry the widow of the man who would have inherited the land. That widow was Ruth. It was the duty of a kinsman-redeemer to buy the land from Naomi, marry Ruth and then the land would be inherited by any children that Ruth gave birth to. The land, however, would still be referred to as belonging to the family of Elimelech. In this way the family name would not disappear. When a man took on the role of kinsman-redeemer, he was actually being very generous.

Naomi had already seen how generous Boaz

was and as she thought about it, God gave her an idea. Boaz was a close relative of her dead husband. Surely he would be their kinsman-redeemer? It would be worth asking. Ruth needed a home of her own. She needed to be well provided for. Boaz must be the answer to all their problems. So one evening, Naomi told Ruth to put on some perfume and dress in the best clothes that she had. 'Go down to the threshing floor. After Boaz has gone to lie down, take note of where he is lying, then go and uncover his feet. He will tell you what to do.'

Ruth did this. And when she uncovered Boaz's feet in the middle of the night, what do you think Boaz felt? At first he felt a bit chilly. The cold night air on his feet woke him and he sat up. Then he got a bit of a fright! After all, it is a bit startling to wake up and find a strange woman sitting at the bottom of your bed!

'Who are you?' he asked.

'I'm Ruth, your servant,' Ruth replied. 'Spread your garment over me since you are my kinsman-redeemer.'

This was Ruth's way of asking Boaz to marry her. Boaz knew what she was asking. He was pleased to be asked, delighted in fact that Ruth had not chosen one of the younger men, but had in fact picked him as a potential husband.

He understood about buying the land from Naomi and about marrying Ruth. He also knew there was another male relative with prior claim to the position of kinsman-redeemer. He would have to be approached first, but Boaz promised to do all that.

'Everyone knows you are of noble character. Stay here until morning. If the other relative is willing, good. If not, as surely as the Lord lives, I will do it.'

Ruth returned to Naomi in the morning with a large sack of grain provided by Boaz and with the news that Boaz was going to look into their situation. Naomi told Ruth to wait and see what would happen. 'Boaz will not rest until the matter is settled today.'

She was right. Boaz immediately went to find the other kinsman-redeemer. The man was willing to buy the land, but was not willing to marry Ruth. So he said to Boaz, 'I cannot do it. You redeem it yourself.'

So Boaz and Ruth were married and later Ruth gave birth to a son whom they called Obed. Naomi was part of their family too. She doted on the little boy so much that the local women would joke amongst themselves, 'Naomi has a son!'

Think about Jesus

Do you remember that amazing name given to Boaz – kinsman-redeemer (see Ruth 3:9 NIV 1984).

A redeemer is someone who buys or takes back something that has been lost. Boaz was Naomi's relative and redeemed her land. He paid her money for the land she could no longer look after. She got money for the land, even though it still belonged to her family. The land was hers, the money was hers. All the cost and all the work was Boaz's. Jesus Christ is the redeemer of sinners. It is by his death that sinners are brought back to peace with God; that peace that was lost through sin. It is by Christ's death that sinners are brought back to the family of God. It is Christ who is the ultimate kinsman-redeemer. He died so that our sins could be forgiven and he rose to life again so that we too can have eternal life. He redeems or brings back sinners to God. We become part of God's family. God is our Father. Naomi and Ruth received protection and family and wealth through their kinsman-redeemer, Boaz. Sinners who trust in God receive forgiveness, salvation and eternal life through their kinsman-redeemer, Jesus Christ. Sinners get all these blessings while all the cost and all the work was Christ's.

Beauty Tips

Here are three other ways to be a Bible Beauty: Patience, kindness and goodness.

Ruth showed patience. It would have been easier for her to stay behind in Moab, but Ruth knew that she must worship the one true God – no matter what the future held. She patiently waited for what God had in store for her whether or not that meant a husband, family or wealth. Glorifying God was all that mattered.

We need to show the same patience in our lives. Being impatient about what the future might hold, does not show others the beauty of God. Ask God to help you be patient and to rejoice in whatever he may bring to your life.

Boaz's kindness to Ruth and Naomi is a small reflection of the much kinder Lord Jesus Christ. At that time in Israel foreigners weren't always looked on with kindness. But Boaz was different. He showed kindness to Ruth who came from the land of Moab. God loves all kinds of people; all tribes and languages. Forgiveness and salvation is for male or female, young or old, any colour. We should show God's love in this way – to people of any nationality or background.

God was so good to Ruth. It might not have seemed so at first when she lost her husband and had to leave her homeland. But God had plans to give her a husband and child, but his plans also went far into the future. Her son Obed was the grandfather of King David. Isn't that amazing? One of the greatest kings of Israel had a refugee as a great-grandmother. And when we look further into the Bible we see the names of Boaz, Ruth, Obed and David in the family tree of Jesus.

Ruth and Boaz were part of God's amazing plan of goodness – a plan to save sinners and give them eternal life. If you trust in Jesus for yourself, reflect God's goodness by showing the people you know and love how good God is. Tell them the good news of Jesus Christ.

GODLY BEAUTY

For God, who said, "Let light shine out of darkness," has shone in our hearts to give the light of the knowledge of the glory of God in the face of Jesus Christ. 2 Corinthians 4:6 (ESV)

When we read about the beauty of God in the Bible a word that we often come across is 'glory'. Whenever we see this word it is telling us how wonderful God is and how we should tell others how wonderful he is. For us to really know God's beauty and glory we must trust Jesus Christ, his Son to forgive us for our sins.

MaRtha aND MaRY

Making sure that your guests feel comfortable in your home is important. But sometimes it doesn't always go to plan. Here are some funny things that have happened to people I know and their guests.

1. The family dog ran off with some underwear.

2. The same dog chased a cat up the chimney.

3. Another dog knocked a mug of coffee over an old lady.

4. Another dog ate the wedding cake.

I think family pets and guests are problematic! Certainly amongst my family and friends! But pets or no pets, the biggest problem is often people. So, let me introduce you to Martha and Mary.

Our two heroines are sisters. Their story shows us the importance of loving God, but how it is also easy for us to forget about God and put ourselves first ... not a beautiful trait at all.

Mary and Martha lived with their brother, Lazarus, in the village of Bethany. One day, Jesus and his disciples visited the area and Martha did what every respectable hostess would do. She invited Jesus and his friends for a meal.

She took charge of things, while Jesus and his companions sat down to talk and relax. Martha started the cooking, getting the ingredients together, all the dishes and drinks, the fruit and the food, the meat, the vegetables, everything that was required. She would have had the fire going in the kitchen to boil things and stew things. She'd have fetched the eggs from the chickens, the milk from the goat, the herbs from the garden. She would have been going here, there and everywhere, just to get it all ready and just so.

While she was doing this, Mary stayed with Jesus and the disciples to listen to what the Lord had to say. He was teaching those who would listen about God his Father. And Mary was listening, eagerly.

This didn't escape Martha's notice, however. With all the boiling and stewing she was getting hot and bothered herself. She was quite flustered with all the extra work she had to do. In a bit of a huff, she decided that enough was enough.

Marching up to Jesus she demanded, 'Lord, do you not care that my sister has left me to serve alone? Tell her then to help me!'

I'm sure you could have heard a pin drop in the moments after Martha's declaration. There must have been quite an awkward atmosphere in the house. Martha had accused Mary, but she had also accused the Lord Jesus. 'Do you not care?' What impertinent words to say to anyone – but especially to Jesus.

Martha obviously didn't really know or understand Jesus. Mary did however. She understood the importance of their guest … she had chosen to stay and listen. Martha had chosen to cook and serve … not bad things … but she'd let herself get flustered, she'd chosen to make a big deal of all that she was doing instead of making a big deal of the one who was a big deal and who was visiting her house – the Son of God.

Well, if a similar situation happened in your home what do you think would happen?

1. Tears and tantrums?

2. Polite conversation and then a quick exit?

3. A firm talking to?

Jesus did give Martha a firm talking to but in a gentle, loving way.

'Martha, Martha, you are anxious and troubled about many things but one thing is necessary. Mary has chosen that good portion which will not be taken away from her.'

These firm, but gentle words were taken to heart by Martha.

She learned her lesson ... the next time she needed Jesus' help, it was a much bigger problem than a few pots and pans. Lazarus, her brother, was very sick.

The news about Lazarus' illness got to Jesus and he could have returned to Bethany in time to heal his friend but he didn't. 'This illness does not lead to death. It is for the glory of God so that the Son of God may be glorified through it,' Jesus told his disciples.

So instead of rushing back to help, he stayed where he was, two more days. When he entered the village, Martha ran out to meet him. 'Lord, if you had been here my brother would not have died. But even now I know that whatever you ask from God, God will give you.

Jesus replied, 'Your brother will rise again.'

Martha said, 'I know that he will rise again on the last day.'

She had been listening to Jesus' teaching. She'd learned her lesson that day when she'd been all flustered in the kitchen. Martha knew that God's people would come back to life and that their souls and bodies would be united once again on the last day.

Jesus wanted to make sure that Martha really understood what this meant. He said to her, 'I am the resurrection and the life. Whoever believes in me, though he dies, yet shall he live and everyone who lives and believes in me shall never die. Do you believe this?'

Martha said, 'Yes Lord, I believe that you are the Christ, the Son of God, who is coming into the world.'

Martha understood that Jesus was the promised Saviour; that he was in fact God! She believed!

Then Martha went to fetch Mary and the two women went with Jesus to the tomb, where Lazarus had been buried. Jesus told some of the mourners to remove the stone from the tomb. Martha was puzzled at this. 'There will be a smell, Lord, for he has been dead for four days.'

Jesus said, 'Did I not tell you that if you believed you would see the glory of God?'

So the stone was removed and Jesus prayed to God, his Father. Then he called, with a loud voice, 'Lazarus, come out!'

And out from the tomb came Lazarus with his hands and feet and face bound up in burial cloths. Jesus told the people to unbind him and let him go.

GODLY BEAUTY

I praise you, for I am fearfully and wonderfully made. Wonderful are your works; my soul knows it very well. Psalm 139:14 (ESV)

The real beauty that we see in the story of Mary and Martha is the beauty of worshipping and believing in the Lord Jesus Christ. If we are true followers of the Lord then we will have a heart like Mary's, one that longs to be with Jesus. People love to gaze on beautiful things. Sometimes we see people staring at pictures for hours. Sometimes we love to go to a particular viewpoint to enjoy the scenery. These are all examples of beautiful things – but they don't or won't last forever. It is the beauty of God that is eternal.

Sometimes we spend so much time on our appearance because we are worried that we are not beautiful. But it is important to understand that you are a creation of God. He made you. The Bible says that we are 'wonderfully made'. It also says that we are made in the image of God. God was pleased when he made humans. It's our sin that has spoiled things. But there is a remedy for sin. Take your sin to God, ask him to forgive you. Jesus died in the place of sinners and that was God's rescue plan from the beginning.

Beauty Tips

Faithfulness: Our God is a faithful God. We can trust him, rely on him, depend on him. Don't doubt our amazing God. He is faithful to us and he gives us the gift of faith. The Bible tells us that this is a free gift. For the amazing gifts of faith and eternal life God charges nothing! Every good and perfect gift comes from God. Real Bible beauty is the same. God gives it to us. It is beautiful to be faithful to the one true and faithful God.

Read More: Ephesians 2:8, Romans 6:23

Think about Jesus

Jesus knew that he was going to raise Lazarus from the dead, but at the graveside he still wept. Jesus was the only one there who knew what life is like without sin and without death. What a beautiful life that must be! How sad Jesus must have been to see that his friend had suffered in this way. Jesus was mourning, not only for the death of his friend, but for the sin of the world. Jesus' love for sinners is so much that he was willing to become sin and be punished for sin even when he hadn't sinned and knew beforehand how terrible sin is and how horrible its punishment would be.

PeRFUMe aND teaRS

hen you have guests to stay, you treat them with respect. Different cultures do this in different ways. Perhaps there is a rule in your family, when you have people over for a meal, that the visitors get served first. Are there rules about things you don't do, when guests come to stay? Look at the following list and pick what you think would be

good ways to welcome a stranger to your home.
Perhaps some of these ideas would not really be
that welcoming?

1. Take their coats and hats.

2. Ask them to sing their favourite song.

3. Offer them a cup of tea and a biscuit.

4. Ask them to bake their favourite cake.

5. Show them somewhere to sit.

6. Ask them how they are feeling.

7. Let them use your trampoline if you have one.

8. Show them your latest dance moves.

9. Teach them your latest dance moves.

10. Play 'Twister' with them.

11. Tickle them.

Now this is probably getting a bit silly, but would
you ever think about ...washing their feet?

Probably not, but in Bible times it would have been a great insult if you had forgotten to wash a guest's feet. The land of Israel was hot and the roads dry and dusty. If a guest had walked through the streets to get to your house, their feet would have been dirty because in those times all you wore on your feet were sandals. So a hospitable host would make sure their guests got a good foot washing.

In this story, of real Bible beauty, look out for the person who washes Jesus' feet, and the person who doesn't.

Have you noticed that not everyone in the Bible has a name? They may have been given a name by their mum and dad but sometimes these names were not written down in the Bible so we don't know what they were really called.

The heroine we are going to read about here is one of those nameless women in the Bible. Some people think that she might have been called Mary Magdalene, a woman that Jesus cast demons out of (see Mark 16:9) and who was one of the first people to witness Jesus' resurrection. However, it's just not certain if that's who this woman really was. Her story is still beautiful though, even if we don't know her name. The story of this sinful but forgiven woman is a story that shows the beauty of God's forgiveness and how beautiful it is to love Jesus.

The story takes place in the house of one of the religious leaders, called Simon. Jesus had been asked to visit Simon's home and as he took his place at the table, a notorious woman of the city entered the house. At that time, if a well-known teacher was going to have a meal at the house of another religious leader or teacher, the public were allowed to come and listen to what they had to say. So that was why this woman was given access to Simon's home. Because of her wicked deeds normally she would never have been allowed in.

When she entered, Jesus was reclining at the table. In Bible times most people didn't use chairs. Instead they lay down on couches or cushions. There would be a table in the middle with all the dishes and goblets to eat and drink from. Each of the diners would lie down on the couches with their heads towards the table and their feet facing away.

When the sinful woman came into the home she brought with her an alabaster jar of ointment. This was very expensive. What she did next was truly amazing. With the tears that were pouring from her eyes, she washed Jesus' feet. She used her long hair to dry them and then she broke open the alabaster box and anointed his feet.

Simon, the religious leader and host, was astonished and said to himself, 'This man, Jesus, claims to be a prophet, but surely if he really was one, he would know who and what this woman really is! She is a sinner!'

Jesus either overheard him, or was able to read his mind. So he said to Simon, 'I've something to say to you.'

'Say it, teacher,' Simon replied.

Then Jesus told Simon a story.

'There was a money lender and two men owed him money. One of the debtors owed 500 silver coins and the other fifty. When these men could not pay the money-lender he cancelled both of their debts. Now which of these debtors will love the money-lender the most?' Jesus asked.

Simon answered, 'The one who had the biggest debt cancelled I suppose.'

Jesus said to him, 'You have judged rightly.' He then turned towards the woman. 'Do you see this woman?' he asked. 'I entered your house; you gave me no water to wash my feet, but she has wet my feet with her tears and wiped them with her hair. You gave me no kiss of greeting, but from the time I came in, she has not ceased to kiss my feet. You did not anoint my head with oil, but she has anointed my feet with ointment. Therefore I tell you her sins, which are many, are forgiven – for she loved much. But he who is forgiven little, loves little.'

Jesus said to the woman, 'Your sins are forgiven. Your faith has saved you. Go in peace.'

Think about Jesus

This is an amazing story. God had shown the sinful woman that she needed forgiveness and she knew that Jesus was the one she had to go to. She knew she was a sinner in great need of salvation. Now, Simon didn't really think much of the woman. Simon thought that he was better than her. He didn't think much of Jesus either – as he hadn't even shown him the most basic hospitality such as washing his feet. Simon didn't realise that even though he was a religious leader, he was a sinner just like the woman. He didn't realise that Jesus was not only a prophet, but the Saviour, the Son of God. Simon didn't love Jesus because he didn't realise how much he needed God's love and forgiveness for his sins. Jesus pointed out Simon's errors through a story. Think about this story yourself. Think about the woman and Simon. Think about the two debtors. Which of them are you like? When you read this story, what is Jesus teaching you about yourself and about God?

BeaUtY TiPS

Here are two more Bible Beauty words: Gentleness and goodness. In this story Jesus was the example of gentleness and goodness. It was certainly not Simon. Remember Simon didn't even wash Jesus' feet. It was the sinful woman who did this. She showed love to Jesus. Jesus showed great love by forgiving the woman for her sins. Sinners don't deserve this love. We deserve God's anger not his gentleness, but God is so gracious, he gives love and forgiveness to his enemies when they repent of their sin and turn to him.

GODLY BEAUTY

Bless those who curse you, pray for those who abuse you. To one who strikes you on the cheek, offer the other also, and from one who takes away your cloak do not withhold your tunic either. Luke 6:28-29 (ESV)

Show the world what Jesus is like by being gentle and good yourself. Ask God to give you gentle words and a gentle spirit. Ask him to help you to treat others in a way that isn't mean or harsh. Ask him to help you be like that to people who may even be mean and harsh to you.

DARLING DORCAS

There's a lot more interest in arts and crafts these days. People are cooking and baking and sewing and there are even television shows that make these skills into competitions. Next we're going to read about a heroine who was well-known for the skill of sewing. So perhaps you should take a minute or two to think of things that you are good at. How could you use that skill to help others? Here are a few different ideas:

1. Are you a good organiser? You could offer your skills to someone who isn't organised. PLEASE COME ROUND TO MY HOUSE!

2. Perhaps you are good at playing games! Well, there are bound to be some mums in church or

100

on your street who might like you to play in the back garden with their kids – while they get on with some chores.

3. Do you like reading stories out loud? How about asking a local nursing home if you can do a story reading session with some old people.

4. Are you good on the computer? How about introducing someone to grocery shopping online, or help them to skype or facetime a relative who lives abroad.

5. Do you like running? If there's someone new in your school or street, become their running buddy or introduce them to your athletics club.

6. Do you like talking to people? How about trying something similar, but different and write a letter to a missionary who is working overseas.

7. Maybe you are an extreme sports fan – well good for you! You can go down a black ski run or

sky dive – and be a missionary while you are at it. Yes! It is true! I really do know people like this!

The Bible tells us to do everything that we do to God's glory.

Read More: 1 Corinthians 10:31

The heroine we are going to read about here showed great love to her friends, neighbours and people who needed her help. The one way she could help was by just doing something that she was good at – and she was good at making clothes.

However, one day Dorcas became ill and died. Her friends were really distressed. They took her body, washed it and laid it out in one of the upstairs rooms. Now Dorcas' home was in the town of Joppa and her Christian friends heard that the apostle Peter was in the town of Lydda not that far away. Dorcas was dead, but they had heard about the amazing things Jesus' disciples were doing after Jesus had come back to life and ascended back to heaven. The disciples were no longer the scaredy-cat bunch of wimps that they had once been. God had given them the power of the Holy Spirit and they were going around preaching the good news and healing people in the name of Jesus Christ.

Dorcas' friends made a decision. 'Let's send for Peter!' So two men headed off for Lydda to fetch him. 'Please come to us without delay,' they pleaded. So Peter got up and went with them. And when he arrived, they took him to the upstairs room.

Dorcas had done so much for so many people. She had shown great love and charity to needy widows. A whole pile of these widows were there at her bedside and they showed Peter the tunics and other garments that Dorcas had made for them, with tears streaming down their faces. She had loved them and they had loved her too. But Peter put all these women outside and knelt down and prayed. Then he turned to the body and said, 'Dorcas, get up!'

Immediately, Dorcas opened her eyes. She was alive! When she saw Peter, she sat up and Peter helped her to get out of bed.

Then he called all her Christian friends and the widows back into the room. Needless to say, the news of Dorcas' resurrection soon spread! It went around all the area of Joppa and many came to believe in Jesus Christ as a result.

Think about Jesus

Dorcas showed others the love of God by doing loving things for them. She used her talents to help those in need. If you love Jesus, show others how loving he is by being caring and helpful – but also by telling them how loving Jesus is. We can show God's love through our actions, but people need to know what Jesus has done. They need to hear it. In fact there is a strange, but beautiful, verse in the Bible that says 'How beautiful are the feet of them that preach the gospel of peace, and bring glad tidings of good things!'

Read More: Isaiah 52:7, Romans 10:15.

Telling others the good news of Jesus Christ is a truly beautiful thing to do. Why does that verse mention feet? Perhaps it's because those who love God don't mind where they go in order to spread the good news of Jesus Christ. Their feet take them to different countries, to dangerous places, to people who don't love God. When they do that, it pleases God – so he tells them their feet are beautiful because they are doing a truly beautiful thing, going and telling others the beautiful truth about salvation.

GODLY BEAUTY

> But the Lord said to Samuel, 'Do not look on his appearance or on the height of his stature, because I have rejected him. For the Lord sees not as man sees: man looks on the outward appearance, but the Lord looks on the heart.'
> 1 Samuel 16:7

Here's an interesting message about beauty from the Bible – and this time it's about a man. The prophet Samuel was told by God to go to the house of Jesse for the one that God had chosen to be the king of Israel was there. When Samuel saw the oldest son, he thought, 'This must be the one that God has chosen.' But it wasn't. God told Samuel 'Do not look on his appearance ... because I have rejected him. Man looks on the outward appearance, but God looks on the heart.' Eventually, David came in from the fields and God said, 'He is the one.' This story tells us what is most important to God – it's not the outside, it's the heart!

BeaUtY TiPS

Last, but not least, in the list of beauty tips is the characteristic of self-control. It means that we control our bodies, minds and souls. We control what goes into our bodies, like food and drink. We're not greedy. We control what goes into our minds, like what we listen to and watch. We focus on God and his Word. We control what comes out of our mouths, like the words that we say. Our words glorify God. But although it is self-control we need God's help to do it. God gives us the fruit of the Spirit when we trust him. That means he gives us: love, joy, peace, patience, kindness, goodness, faithfulness, gentleness and self-control! Use God's Word as your life mirror – and remember that it's these words, God's Word, that show real beauty!

Read More: Galatians 5:19-26

RUBY AND YOU

Now there isn't really a woman in the Bible called Ruby, but the Bible tells us in Proverbs that a truly good woman is worth far more than rubies. And the writer in Proverbs describes what this woman is like. She's energetic, skilful, busy, creative, organised. She may sound too good to be true ... but wait a minute before you judge her too harshly.

First of all here's a question for you: If you were describing how valuable someone was, what possessions or precious items would you use to show how valuable that person was to you?

Might you say:

1. You are more precious to me than my mobile phone?

2. You are more valuable to me than a pair of diamond encrusted shoes?

3. You are more treasured than a hundred bursting bank accounts?

I'm sure you can think of quite a few more imaginative ideas.

The woman in Proverbs 31 is described as being like rubies. You can't get more precious than that. Rubies are pretty expensive.

The writer of Proverbs describes this virtuous woman as being worth even more than rubies, not because she is stunning or rich, but because she has characteristics that he holds in high esteem. She is hard-working. She doesn't just sit at home and do nothing. She even runs her own business. She's described as physically strong because she's up and about early in the morning and working until late at night. She provides clothing and food for her family and she looks out for the needs of others. The Bible describes her clothing as strength and honour. Now that would be a strange thing to read in a fashion magazine wouldn't it?

This year's 'must have' item in your wardrobe: a finely cut designer suit called Honour.

On the catwalk this spring: a nifty little number called Strength.

That's not how the world thinks. But this is how we should be. Because strength and honour are worth far more than pastel this and trendy that.

Remember how the Bible says that beauty is passing. These words come from Proverbs 31:30.

'Charm is deceitful and beauty is passing but a woman who fears the Lord, she shall be praised.'

Strength and honour are two great blessings, but the ultimate description of godly beauty is what you've just read from the Bible: the fear of the Lord.

This fear is not the same fear you get when you are in danger, or when you think you are in danger. This fear is nothing to do with spiders or fire or even roller-coasters. (Take your pick of other scary things that make your hands sweat.)

This fear, the fear of the Lord, is different. It means that we are to show all honour and respect to God. We are to respond to his love by loving him back. And any fear that we have should be a fear of not loving him, of not pleasing him, of not giving him the respect that he deserves.

Show your fear or great respect to God by:

Love. Love God because he first loved you.

Joy. Be joyful in all circumstances. Be joyful in God's presence.

Peace. Be at peace with your creator by submitting to his will.

Patience. Be patient as you wait for God's purposes to be fulfilled. His timing is perfect.

Kindness. Be kind to others. Be generous.

Goodness. Be good by obeying God's Word.

Faithfulness. Be faithful and loyal to the one who planned your salvation. Don't give in to the demands of the world. Stay strong by trusting in God and being grounded in his Word.

Gentleness. Use gentle words and actions. Be gentle in order to show others how beautiful and gentle our loving, all powerful, God is.

Self-control. Show self-control by putting God and others first. Christ, the King of kings, put others before himself. When you want something you don't always need it. You shouldn't always get what you want. Ask God to help you want what he wants.

The Bible is so full of wisdom and godly truth, and it has some really good advice for young girls and women.

Take God's Word and live by it. Listen to it being preached by those who love God's word and obey it.

Make sure you listen to older, godly women who have lived as Christians and have read God's Word. Heed their advice. In the book of Titus chapter 2, the Apostle Paul wrote to a young man called Titus who needed advice about how to run a church. Paul encouraged him to have the older women help out the younger women.

They were to tell the young women to love their husbands and children (good advice for you if and when that time comes!) But they were also to be discreet, pure, and live in such a way that the Word of God would be honoured.

As you read God's word and take advice from godly, older women, remember that one day you will be called on to do the same thing. Even if you get married or not, as a follower of Christ you should become someone who will help others to learn about God and obey him.

Get ready for this

future part

of your life now. Do this by living a life of prayer, nourishing your soul with the Word of God so that in the years to come, you will be able to give God's good advice to others.

There is an advert you might have seen on television for a brand of make-up. The slogan says, 'Because you're worth it.' The marketing team want you to buy that brand of make-up by making you think you deserve the best.

Well, whether you buy it or not – that's not the real reason I'm mentioning that slogan. 'Worth it.'

Who is worth it? What do we really deserve? As a sinner you deserve God's anger, but God wants to show you his love instead. He takes no joy in the death of the wicked. He offers you salvation. If you refuse it then you will get what you deserve.

Read More: Ezekiel 33:11

Jesus took the punishment of sin. He suffered

greatly by leaving the perfection and glory of heaven to live a life on this sinful earth. What God has done through Christ means that salvation is offered freely to undeserving sinners.

Accept God's offer of salvation. Trust in him and devote your life to worshipping him. Give your heart to God. Spend your life showing the world how beautiful Christ is – because: Jesus is worth it!

What is a Princess?

hat would you do if you woke up one morning to discover that overnight you'd become a princess?

Would you:

a) Jump out of bed and rush to your super-sized wardrobe chock-a-block with bling! Try on Monday morning's tiara and send off an order for some diamond-studded shoes to match?

b) Shout 'Off with their heads!' – just for the practice?

c) Check on all the handsome princes out there?

d) Curtsey to your mother and then write a list, checking it twice, about all the really good causes you're going to support?

If you answered a) – watch out for a revolution; your crazy spending habits will not make your subjects like you.

If you answered b) – watch out for a revolution; chopping off people's heads will not make your subjects like you. Not at all.

If you answered c) – Watch out for a revolution; the ugly princes might be offended.

If you answered d) – you're safe! Phew! You're such a nice all-round good-girl princess that all the revolutionaries will just love you!

With all that talk of revolutions, perhaps you've changed your mind about being a princess. It might not be the best career choice. Perhaps being a princess is not all it's cracked up to be. Is the life of a princess all about jewels and dances? Could it be about wars and battles too?

Being a princess is certainly a life of privilege

and power – for some it is a great life. But the princesses we're going to read about don't quite fit the glitzy-ditzy image that some imagine is the life of a royal princess. In this book we have princesses who showed just as much bravery as warriors – yet they didn't carry swords. We also have princesses who were sharp thinkers – women who made wise decisions. And we've got quite a few princesses who did the wisest thing of all – trust in God.

You see, all these princesses are from the Bible – and that is something that should make you sit up and take notice. God has put these women in his Word for a reason – and you need to find out why.

But not all the princesses in this book are heroines. Some of the royal ladies in the Bible were lean mean killing machines – the bad princesses of the Bible. Yeah, watch out for those girls! One of them comes to a particularly grizzly end – not good if you're feeling a bit squeamish.

'Hang on a second,' I hear you say. 'This book is How to be a Bible princess. What do you mean exactly? Can I be a princess?'

Good question. Here's the deal. Unless you're born in a royal family, or marry a prince, you're not going to be a princess. But you can join a royal family – THE royal family – God's family. Being part of God's family is not about birth or status or if you've got a crown or two in your cupboard. It's not about what you look like, or about being in charge. It's not even about being the nicest, most organised, generous person around. Being a Bible princess is about being part of the true royal family that has God the Father, God the Son and God the Holy Spirit at its centre. It's a family that anyone can enter into if they trust in the Lord Jesus Christ to save them from their sins.

If you trust in Jesus to save you from sin you are something even better than a worldly princess, you are a child of God. Your Creator has made you – a girl – and he has saved you – a sinner. And one day you will be perfect, privileged and beautiful beyond imagination. That's what being a Bible princess is all about. It's really about being a child of God. A sinner saved by God's grace. When you trust in Jesus, the wrong things that you've done are wiped away because of God's love, power and wonderful mercy. Read on and find out more about how you can be part of the true royal family ... God's family!

Who is
Catherine Mackenzie?

I live in the Highlands of Scotland, in a town called Inverness. I have loads of nieces and nephews and some of them have red hair like me. As a young girl, I was an avid reader and I still am. The only way my parents could persuade me to take my medicine was to 'bribe' me with a book.

When I grew up a little, I remember being allowed to read in bed for an extra half hour and thinking it was the best thing ever.

In school, I loved to write stories in class, though my spelling was more than a bit wobbly. However, that wasn't the worst mistake I made at that age. It took some time for me to realise that I was a sinner and that I needed Jesus to save me.

I thought I was good enough for God. I wasn't. When I became an older teen, I realised that the Lord Jesus died to save me from my sin.

That was when I found something life-changing to write about – the Word of God; Jesus Christ; Salvation – the topics are endless.

I started by writing articles for our church newspaper and finally wrote my first book when I was in my twenties. I was asked to write a biography about a man called Richard Wurmbrand. And since then, writing true life stories has been a major part of my life.

The main reason I write, is because there is a wonderful true life story that has given my life real meaning – the life, death and resurrection of my Lord Jesus Christ. Of all the heroes and heroines I've written about, he is the best.

HOW TO BE A BIBLE PRINCESS

BIBLE PRINCESS

Catherine MacKenzie

If you were a princess you'd have the best

wardrobe in the world with new dresses in it

every day - and a tiara to match. But is that all

there is to being a princess? And what does

it mean to be a real Bible princess? Abigail,

Jehosheba, Esther, The Queen of the South,

Pharaoh's daughter, Michal, Jezebel and

Herodias' daughter are all Bible Princesses –

good and bad. Find out what their stories can

teach you about being a child of God.

ISBN 978-1-84550-825-8

This book is a wonderful book for anyone wanting to
provide a young girl with wholesome reading while
reinforcing biblical values. My daughter enjoys hearing
about ' real princesses' and I like that it is getting her
interested in the Bible.
Train Up a Child Mom

CHRISTIAN FOCUS PUBLICATIONS

Christian Focus | Christian Heritage | CF4K | Mentor

Christian Focus Publications publishes books for adults and children under its four main imprints: Christian Focus, CF4K, Mentor and Christian Heritage. Our books reflect our conviction that God's Word is reliable and Jesus is the way to know him, and live for ever with him.

Our children's publication list includes a Sunday School curriculum that covers pre-school to early teens, and puzzle and activity books. We also publish personal and family devotional titles, biographies and inspirational stories that children will love.

If you are looking for quality Bible teaching for children then we have an excellent range of Bible stories and age-specific theological books.

From pre-school board books to teenage apologetics, we have it covered!

Find us at our web page:
www.christianfocus.com

CF4•K
Because you're never too young to know Jesus